ISBN 1 85854 368 1
© Brimax Books Ltd 1996. All rights reserved.
Published by Brimax Books Ltd, Newmarket,
CB8 7AU, England 1996.
Printed in France - n°67820-C

Off to School

by Gill Davies
Illustrated by Stephanie Longfoot

BRIMAX • NEWMARKET • ENGLAND

Going to school is exciting.
Today is our first day.

We put our coats and shoes on.
Now at last we are on our way.

Our mother and the baby
Walk with us down the street.

"We are going to school today,"
We say to everyone we meet.

Mother takes us into school.
There are lots of children there.

A smiling lady talks to us.
We stand and look and stare.

We feel a little funny
When Mother says goodbye.

The baby waves her hand
And we wonder, will we cry?

But then the smiling lady
Who says her name is Mrs New,

Gives us both a little hug
And shows us lots of things to do.

There are lots of blocks to build with,
And a sandbox and a slide;

Paint to paint and songs to sing
And a tricycle to ride.

Mrs New reads us a story
About a puppy and his bone.

She shows us all the pictures.
Then we draw some of our own.

Then suddenly it's time to go.
"Your mother's here," says Mrs New.

We ask, "Can we come again tomorrow?
There are lots of things to do."